BIGGEST ANIMALS

That's Wild!
A Look at Animals

Big Buddy BOOKS
That's Wild!

ABDO
Publishing Company

Julie Murray

VISIT US AT
www.abdopublishing.com

Published by ABDO Publishing Company, 8000 West 78th Street, Edina, Minnesota 55439.

Copyright © 2010 by Abdo Consulting Group, Inc. International copyrights reserved in all countries. No part of this book may be reproduced in any form without written permission from the publisher. Buddy Books™ is a trademark and logo of ABDO Publishing Company.

Printed in the United States of America, North Mankato, Minnesota.
112009
012010

 PRINTED ON RECYCLED PAPER

Coordinating Series Editor: Rochelle Baltzer
Editor: Sarah Tieck
Contributing Editors: Heidi M.D. Elston, Megan M. Gunderson, BreAnn Rumsch, Marcia Zappa
Graphic Design: Deborah Coldiron, Maria Hosley
Cover Photograph: *Eighth Street Studio*; *iStockphoto*: ©iStockphoto.com/Rouzes; *Shutterstock*: Robert Hardhout.
Interior Photographs/Illustrations: *Amazing Creatures CD*: Stockbyte (pp. 5, 13); *AnimalsAnimals - Earth Scenes*: ©Cranston, Bob (p. 23), ©OSF/Fleetham, D (p. 26); *AP Photo*: Sergei Grits (p. 15); *Eighth Street Studio* (pp. 7, 9, 15, 18, 23, 24, 30); *iStockphoto*: ©iStockphoto.com/ikachan76 (p. 8), ©iStockphoto.com/Jbryson (p. 17), ©iStockphoto.com/jpll2002 (p. 10), ©iStockphoto.com/lingbeck (p. 5), ©iStockphoto.com/mammamaart (p. 29), ©iStockphoto.com/merrilld (p. 10), ©iStockphoto.com/ranplett (p. 29); *Minden Pictures*: Flip Nicklin (pp. 24, 26); *Peter Arnold, Inc.*: ©BIOS Bios-Auteurs (droits geres)Montford Thierry (pp. 5, 17), ©Biosphoto/Colla Phillip/Visual and Written (p. 20), ©Biosphoto/Crocetta Tony (p. 17), WILDLIFE (pp. 19, 26); *Shutterstock*: Paul Banton (p. 7), Craig Barhorst (p. 23), Jill Battaglia (p. 29), dirkr (p. 8), Mike Donenfeld (p. 15), EcoPrint (p. 5), Four Oaks (p.13), javarman (p. 8), Joe Mercier (p. 29).

Library of Congress Cataloging-in-Publication Data

Murray, Julie, 1969-
 Biggest animals / Julie Murray.
   p. cm. -- (That's wild! : a look at animals)
 ISBN 978-1-60453-976-9
 1. Body size--Juvenile literature. I. Title.
 QL799.3.M87 2010
 590--dc22
                                2009033005

Contents

Wildly Big!

Many amazing animals live in our world. Some are fast and others are slow. They may fly, run, or swim.

Some animals are wildly big! Being large can help them survive in their **habitats**. Their size might help them get food. Or, it may scare off predators. Let's learn more about big animals!

Whale Shark

Pacific Ocean

Giant Anaconda

4

Big animals live all over the world. The same type of animal may live in several parts of the world.

North America

Atlantic Ocean

Europe

Asia

Pacific Ocean

Africa

South America

Ostriches

Giraffes

African Elephant

5

Seeing Treetops

Giraffes are the world's tallest land animals. Male giraffes can be 18 feet (5 m) tall and weigh as much as 3,000 pounds (1,360 kg)! Females can be 14 feet (4 m) tall and can weigh 2,600 pounds (1,180 kg). Giraffes are as tall as some trees!

Giraffes live in Africa in grassy areas called savannas. They eat plants. One of their favorite meals is acacia tree leaves.

Head Bangers

Giraffes have small horns on top of their heads. Males use them to bump heads during fights.

A giraffe's spit is thick and gooey. This protects its tongue as it eats leaves off thorny treetops.

All giraffes have a long neck and very long legs. A giraffe's legs can be six feet (2 m) long. This is taller than some adult men!

Being tall allows a giraffe to munch on leaves from tall trees. And, it helps a giraffe spot predators before they get close.

To reach water, giraffes spread and bend their legs. They get most of their water from their food. So, they don't need to drink very often!

Off-road trucks are big. Some weigh more than 5,000 pounds (2,270 kg). But, an African elephant can weigh three times that!

Now You Know

African and Asian elephants are similar, but African elephants are bigger.

More to Love

African elephants are huge animals! Males can weigh about 15,000 pounds (6,800 kg). This makes them the world's heaviest land animal. And at about 11 feet (3 m) tall, they are the second-tallest land animal.

Elephants eat a lot. Adults take in about 300 pounds (140 kg) of food every day. This includes grass, leaves, and fruit. Elephants also drink about 40 gallons (150 L) of water every day.

11

Like giraffes, African elephants live in Africa. This is a very warm **habitat**. So, these giants have special features to survive in the heat.

To stay cool, African elephants flap their large, gray ears. This allows extra body heat to escape. And, they use their trunks to take cold showers.

A baby elephant is called a calf. Calves have short trunks, so their mothers spray them to cool them off.

13

Big Bird

Ostriches are the world's largest birds. Males weigh more than 220 pounds (100 kg). And, they stand seven to nine feet (2 to 3 m) tall. That is taller than most grown men!

Even though ostriches can't fly, they run very fast. Sometimes, they reach 43 miles (69 km) per hour. When ostriches run, one step can move them more than ten feet (3 m)!

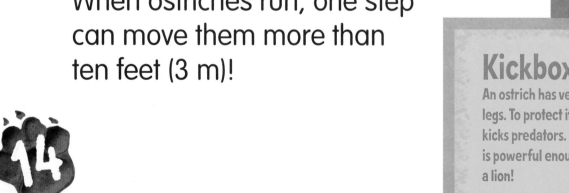

Kickboxer

An ostrich has very strong legs. To protect itself, it kicks predators. Its kick is powerful enough to kill a lion!

Wild ostriches live on the plains and deserts of Africa.
In other parts of the world, farmers raise ostriches.

15

Hold On!

The giant anaconda is the world's largest snake. Giant anacondas can be about 30 feet (9 m) long and 12 inches (30 cm) thick! They can weigh around 500 pounds (230 kg).

Giant anacondas eat big animals, such as deer, turtles, and jaguars. They use their strong **muscles** to squash their **prey** to death. Then, they open their mouths very wide and swallow the animal whole!

Giant anacondas live in South America in streams, swamps, and marshes. They can move quickly in the water.

Giant anacondas are olive green with black spots. So, they are also known as green anacondas.

Did You Know?
Female giant anacondas are larger than males.

17

Under the Sea

Open Wide!
Whale sharks have about 3,000 tiny teeth!

Many large fish live underwater. The largest is the whale shark. It can be 40 feet (12 m) long.

Sharks are known for attacking **prey** with their sharp teeth. But, whale sharks are gentle giants. They swim with their mouths wide open to catch food. They eat **plankton** and small fish.

Whale sharks live around the world in tropical oceans. Tropical areas are warm.

19

Ocean sunfish are odd-looking creatures. Their tail never fully grows, so they look like only half a fish! And, they are unable to fully close their mouths.

Ocean sunfish live in warm ocean waters. They swim near the water's surface, where the sun warms them.

Ocean sunfish are the world's heaviest bony fish. They can weigh more than 4,000 pounds (1,810 kg)!

These unusual fish have flat, oval-shaped bodies. The largest ocean sunfish can measure more than ten feet (3 m) long!

From the Deep

Giant squid live deep in the ocean. These long, slender **invertebrates** are among the ocean's largest creatures. They can measure 60 feet (18 m) long!

In 2007, fishermen caught a different large squid. They called it the colossal squid. Colossal squid live very deep in the ocean. So, they are hard to study. But, some scientists believe they may be even larger than giant squid!

An average school bus is about 40 feet (12 m) long. Giant squid can grow to be the length of a bus and a half!

I've Got My Eye on You!

A giant squid eye can be as large as a basketball!

SCHOOL BUS

STOP

Squid use their long, armlike tentacles to catch prey. Most squid eat fish, shrimp, and other squid.

23

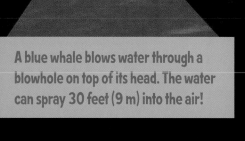

A blue whale blows water through a blowhole on top of its head. The water can spray 30 feet (9 m) into the air!

No Way!

At certain times of the year, a blue whale eats more than four tons (4 t) of food each day! It eats tiny, shrimplike creatures called krill.

World's Largest

Whales are among the world's largest creatures. The blue whale is the biggest type of whale. It is also the biggest animal in the world!

Human
Average Height: 6 feet (2 m)

Bottlenose Dolphin
Average Length: 9–13 feet (3–4 m)

Killer Whale
Average Length: 18–32 feet (5–10 m)

Humpback Whale
Average Length: 35–50 feet (11–15 m)

Bowhead Whale
Average Length: 49–60 feet (15–18 m)

Sperm Whale
Average Length: 36–59 feet (11–18 m)

Blue Whale
Average Length: 82–85 feet (25–26m)

Blue whales live in all of Earth's oceans. Sometimes, they can be seen swimming near the water's surface.

Blue whales have giant bodies. The largest ones can be more than 90 feet (27 m) long! An adult blue whale can weigh more than 150 tons (136 t). Its heart alone can weigh as much as a small car!

That WAS wild!

From tall giraffes to giant blue whales, there are some very big wild animals. Each of them is an important part of the animal kingdom.

People work hard to **protect** animals and their surroundings. You can help, too! Recycling and using less water are two simple things you can do. The more you learn, the more you can do to help keep animals safe.

Important Words

habitat a place where a living thing is naturally found.

invertebrate (ihn-VUHR-tuh-bruht) an animal without a backbone.

muscles (MUH-suhls) body tissues, or layers of cells, that help move the body.

plankton tiny animals and plants that float in a body of water.

prey an animal hunted or killed by a predator for food.

protect (pruh-TEHKT) to guard against harm or danger.

Web Sites

To learn more about big animals, visit ABDO Publishing Company online. We
about big animals are featured on our Book Links page. These links are routinely
and updated to provide the most current information available.

www.abdopublishing.com

Index